YOU ARE THE

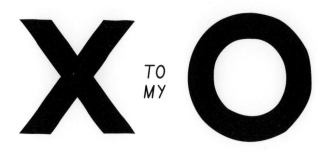

X TO MY O

A BOOK FOR MY OTHER HALF

GWION PRYDDERCH

KNOCK KNOCK®
LOS ANGELES, CALIFORNIA

TO _____

FROM _____

YOU ARE...

THE SPRINKLES

TO MY DOUGHNUT

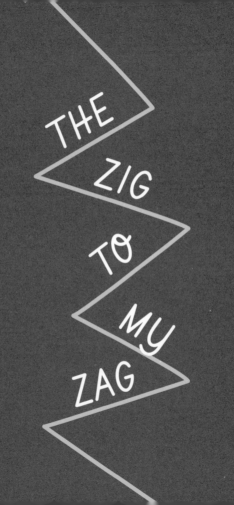

THE WI

TO MY FI

THE
SLEEVE
TO MY
CUP

TO MY TOOTHPASTE

THE A-SIDE

TO MY B-SIDE

THE DIP

TO MY CHIPS

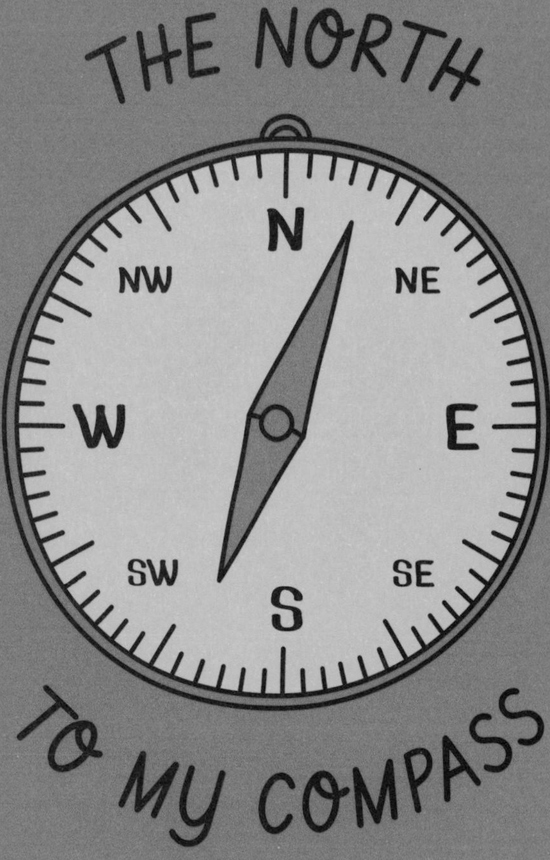
THE NORTH
N
NW
NE
W
E
SW
SE
S
TO MY COMPASS

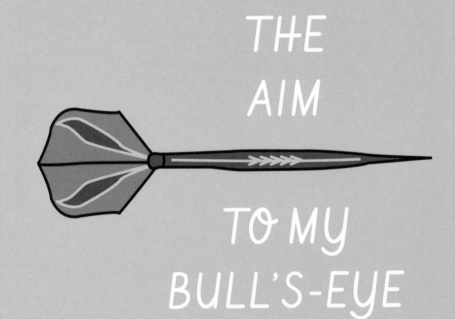

THE
AIM

TO MY
BULL'S-EYE

THE CUT TO MY PASTE

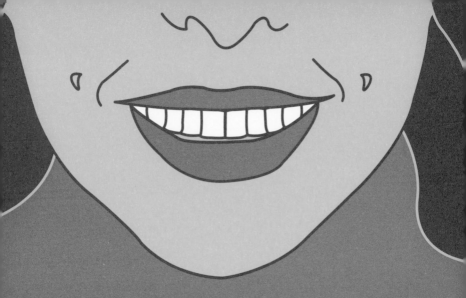

THE DIMPLES
TO MY SMILE

TO MY
GRILLED
CHEESE

THE ABRA
TO MY
CADABRA

THE 🙈 TO MY 😻

THE LACES
TO MY SNEAKERS

THE FISH

TO MY CHIPS

THE

TO MY
POWERS

THE

JUMP

TO MY

BATTERY

THE BASS

TO MY TREBLE

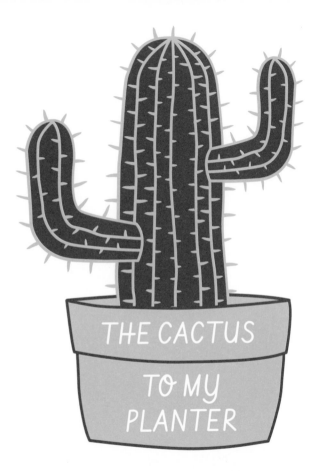

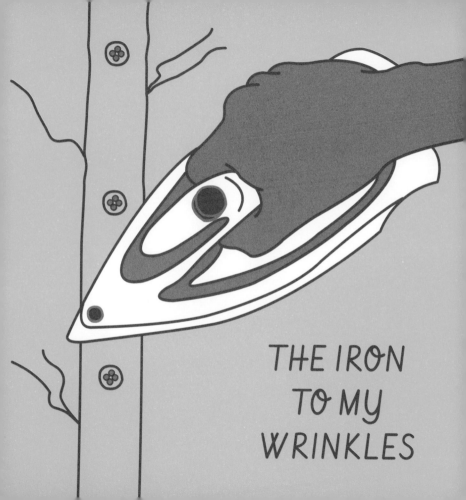

THE IRON
TO MY
WRINKLES

THE

TORTOISE

TO

MY

HARE

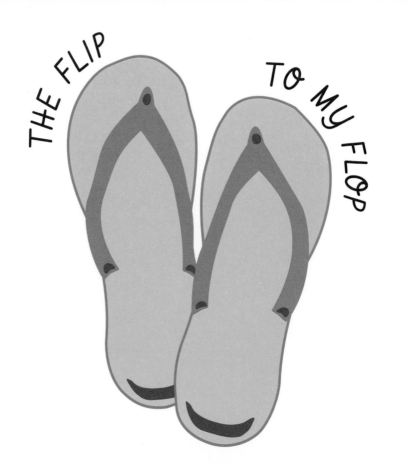

THE WINNING NUMBERS

(2) (3) (17) (21) (14) (13)

TO MY
LOTTERY TICKET

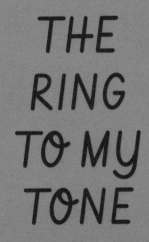

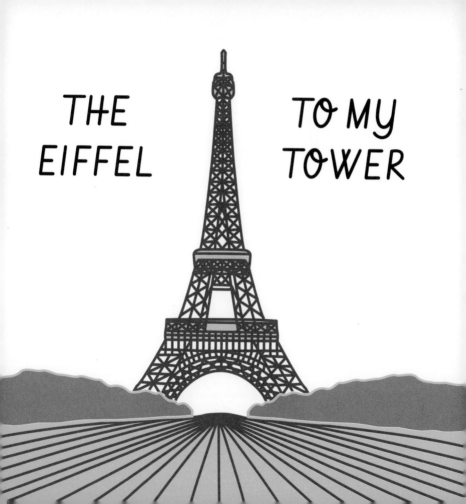

THE PING

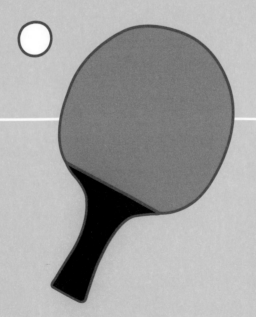

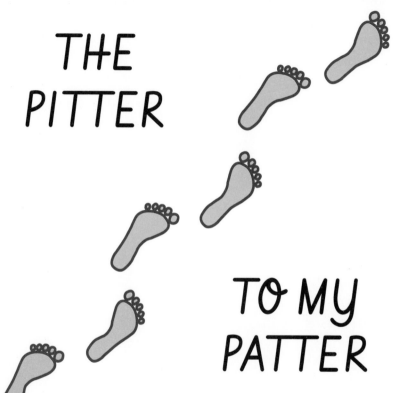

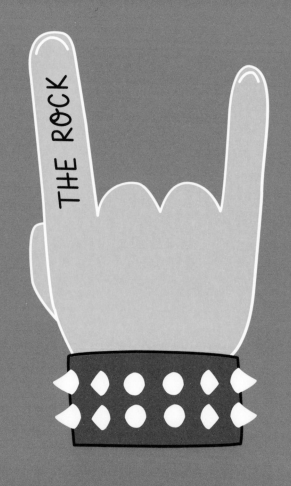

THE SEA
TO MY SHELL

THE MARSHMALLOWS

TO MY S'MORES

THE SPRING TO MY STEP

THE
CHECK

TO MY
MATE

TO MY COASTER

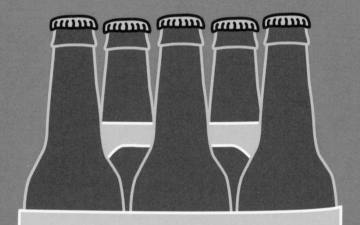

THE HOPS
TO MY BEER

THE
STRING
TO MY
BALLOON

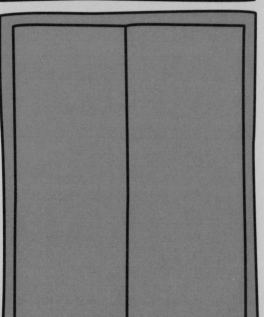

TO MY DOWN

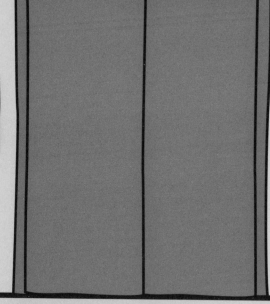

THE 21

TO MY
BLACKJACK

THE PEN TO MY PAPER

THE WANDER

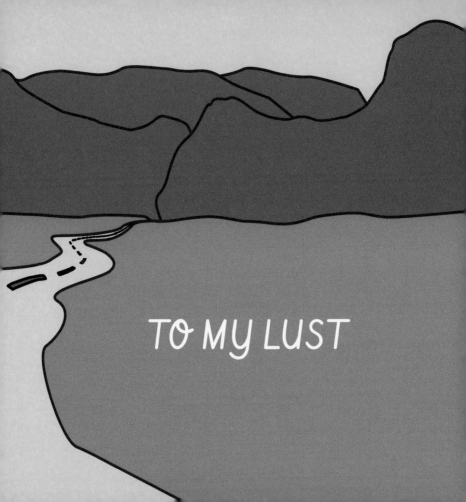

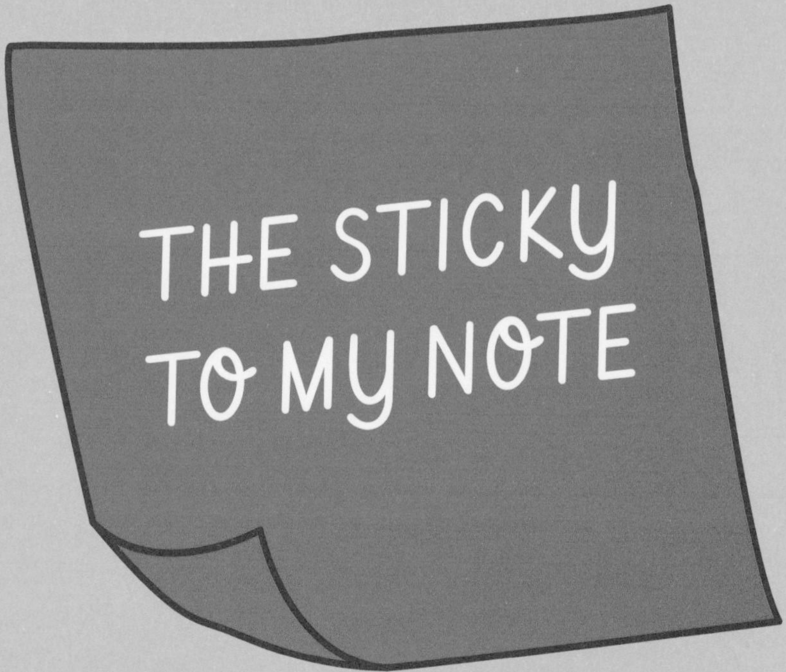
THE STICKY
TO MY NOTE

THE PICK

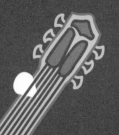

TO MY
GUITAR

TO MY BATH

THE BEES
TO MY
KNEES

THE TURN

TO MY NEXT PAGE

THE

SURPRISE!

TO MY PARTY

THE
FIVE STARS

TO MY
REVIEW

THE SKYLINE

THE NEXT EPISODE

TO MY CLIFF-HANGER

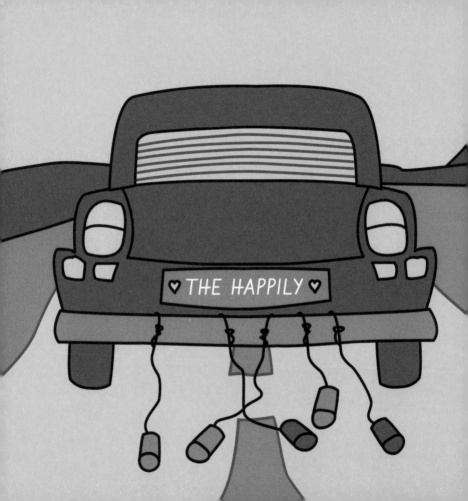

TO MY
EVER AFTER

Published and distributed by Knock Knock
6080 Center Drive
Los Angeles, CA 90045
knockknockstuff.com
Knock Knock is a registered trademark of Knock Knock LLC

Conceived, designed, and illustrated by Gwion Prydderch

This book is meant solely for entertainment purposes. In no event will Knock Knock be liable to any reader for any harm, injury, or damages, including direct, indirect, incidental, special, consequential, or punitive arising out of or in connection with the use of the information contained in this book. So there.

ISBN: 978-1-68349-224-5
UPC: 825703-50217-6

10 9 8 7 6 5 4 3 2 1